21st Century Skills Library

HEALTH AT RISK

ALCOHOL

Lydia Bjornlund

Cherry Lake Publishing
Ann Arbor, Michigan

CHERRY LAKE
Publishing

Published in the United States of America by Cherry Lake Publishing
Ann Arbor, Michigan
www.cherrylakepublishing.com

Content Advisor: Carolyn Walker, RN, PhD, Professor, School of Nursing, San Diego State University, San Diego, California

Photo Credits: Cover and page 1, © Philip Lewis/Alamy; page 4, AP Images/Eric Risberg; page 7, AP Images/University of Florida, Ray Carson; page 9, © Jupiter Images/Brand X/William Fritsch/Alamy; page 11, © Galina Barskaya/Shutterstock; page 12, Maury Aaseng; page 14, © Bruce Liron/Alamy; page 16, © Vova Pomortzeff; page 18, © Tad Denson/Shutterstock; page 19, © Grantly Lynch/Alamy; page 22, © Tomi/Photo Link/Alamy; page 23, Kitch Bain/Shutterstock; page 25, © Photodisc/SW Productions/Alamy; page 26, AP Images/The Hawkeye, John Lovretta; page 29, © Photodisc/SW Productions/Alamy

Library of Congress Cataloging-in-Publication Data
Bjornlund, Lydia D.
Alcohol / Lydia Bjornlund.
p. cm.—(Health at risk)
ISBN-13: 978-1-60279-280-7
ISBN-10: 1-60279-280-1
1. Alcohol—Health aspects—Juvenile literature. 2. Alcoholism—Juvenile literature. I. Title. II. Series.
RA1242.A35B56 2008
613.81—dc22 2008017495

Cherry Lake Publishing would like to acknowledge the work of The Partnership for 21st Century Skills.
Please visit www.21stcenturyskills.org *for more information.*

Table of Contents

CHAPTER ONE

The World of Alcohol

A vendor sells beer at a San Francisco Giants game. Many fans associate sporting events with drinking alcohol.

Alcoholic drinks have existed since ancient times. Long ago, people learned to make beer, wine, and **spirits**. They made these drinks from **fermented** fruits and grains. Alcoholic drinks were used as medicine and in social settings.

Today, alcohol flows freely at many events. Beer is sold to the fans in the stands at ball games. Weddings and other special events are celebrated with a champagne toast. In some cultures, business deals are sealed with a drink. You see adults drinking beer at the local park. You see people sipping a glass of wine with dinner at a fancy restaurant. You may sit with your parents as they relax with a **cocktail** before dinner. You might even have a friend who's snuck a sip of alcohol.

It is important to remember that alcohol is a **drug**. Like other drugs, alcohol affects your body quickly. It also has long-lasting effects. Alcohol goes directly into your bloodstream and slows down your brain. People often like the relaxed feeling they get from a drink or two. But even small amounts of alcohol can cause unpleasant effects. Many people who have been drinking cannot walk straight or keep their balance. They feel dizzy, and their eyesight gets blurry.

This is why drinking and driving is a bad idea. In 2006, over 17,600 people died in alcohol-related traffic crashes in the United States. In Canada, 38 percent of drivers killed in automobile crashes had been drinking alcohol. And the majority of these drivers (almost 85 percent) had **blood alcohol content** above the legal limit.

Learning & Innovation Skills

Images of drinking on television and in movies and magazines make alcohol seem cool. Beer commercials show healthy people out having fun. Advertisers—and the companies they work for—create these images. They want to appeal to your emotions, not to your brain. Experts say you can get smart about media messages by asking yourself questions: Who is sending the message? Who are they trying to reach? What is the purpose of the ad? How does the ad try to achieve that purpose? How does the ad affect your opinion about the alcoholic product?

A student at the University of Florida attempts an exercise meant to simulate drunk driving. Wearing goggles that simulate the symptoms of an alcohol-impaired driver, she tries to drive a remote control car.

21st Century Content

In many places and times, people have opposed alcohol use. In the 1800s, Americans began to protest the use of alcohol, saying that it led to public drunkenness, fights, and violence. They said that people who drink were less responsible. In 1919, the Eighteenth Amendment to the U.S. Constitution outlawed the manufacture or sale of alcohol throughout the country. This 20-year period was known as **Prohibition**.

It was impossible to enforce the new law, however. Illegal manufacturers and bars grew up in cities and towns across America. In 1933, Congress repealed Prohibition with the Twenty-first Amendment.

People who drink too much often have little control over their emotions too. They might be happy one minute and crying or angry the next. They might become mean or violent. They often say and do things they don't mean.

It is likely that someone someday will ask you if you want a drink. By knowing the risks, you will be able to make a good decision.

CHAPTER TWO

The Effects of Alcohol

A young man is arrested for drunk driving. In spite of the many penalties given to drunk drivers, people continue to take the risks.

Jeff, who is 17, says he had "way too many" beers, tequila shots, and drinks of whiskey at a friend's party. He doesn't remember stumbling out the door after the party. He

21st Century Content

Alcohol slows down reaction times and the ability to make decisions. This is why it is so dangerous to drive after drinking. In the United States, there is an average of one alcohol-related traffic fatality every 30 minutes. People who are caught driving drunk sometimes receive warnings or fines. Sometimes they lose their licenses for a few months. In extreme cases, they might go to jail. Some people think we should have stricter punishments for people who are caught driving under the influence of alcohol. Others say that the only way to reduce drunk driving is to educate people about the dangers. What do you think would work best?

doesn't remember vomiting in the bushes or falling asleep in the backseat of a car. The next thing he remembers is seeing the police car's flashing lights when police woke him up.

Drinking too much can make you sick. Like Jeff, you might vomit. You might not remember what happened. You might say and do things that you regret and would not do sober. You also might wake up the next day feeling awful. This is called a **hangover**. A hangover is your body's way of telling you that you drank too much alcohol.

Alcohol can cause far more serious problems than simply feeling awful. The use of alcohol increases problems

Alcohol abuse is particularly worrisome because it can lead to so many physical and mental problems.

in school. It contributes to fights and criminal behavior. Each year, millions of teens are admitted to the hospital after drinking too much. Each year, hundreds of college students die as a result of accidents, violence, or **alcohol poisoning** linked to alcohol consumption.

Alcohol can create long-term

Learning & Innovation Skills

How much alcohol is too much? This is difficult to determine because alcohol does not affect all people in the same way. In general, women are more affected by alcohol than men. Thin people are more affected than heavier people. It is hard to predict the effects of alcohol. How alcohol is absorbed in the body depends on several factors. Body weight, body type, general health and liver function, how fast you drink, and how much and what you have eaten all play a part.

Alcohol Impairment Chart

Men

Approximate Blood Alcohol Percentage

Drinks	100	120	140	160	180	200	220	240	Body Weight in Pounds
0	.00	.00	.00	.00	.00	.00	.00	.00	Only Safe Driving Limit
1	.04	.03	.03	.02	.02	.02	.02	.02	Impairment Begins
2	.08	.06	.05	.05	.04	.04	.03	.03	Driving Skills Affected Possible Criminal Penalties
3	.11	.09	.08	.07	.06	.06	.05	.05	
4	.15	.12	.11	.09	.08	.08	.07	.06	
5	.19	.16	.13	.12	.11	.09	.09	.08	
6	.23	.19	.16	.14	.13	.11	.10	.09	
7	.26	.22	.19	.16	.15	.13	.12	.11	Legally Intoxicated
8	.30	.25	.21	.19	.17	.15	.14	.13	
9	.34	.28	.24	.21	.19	.17	.15	.14	Criminal Penalties
10	.38	.31	.27	.23	21	.19	.17	.16	

Women

Approximate Blood Alcohol Percentage

Drinks	90	100	120	140	160	180	200	220	240	Body Weight in Pounds
0	.00	.00	.00	.00	.00	.00	.00	.00	.00	Only Safe Driving Limit
1	.05	.05	.04	.03	.03	.03	.02	.02	.02	Impairment Begins
2	.10	.09	.08	.07	.06	.05	.05	.04	.04	Driving Skills Affected Possible Criminal Penalties
3	.15	.14	.11	.10	.09	.06	.07	.06	.06	
4	.20	.18	.15	.13	.11	.10	.09	.06	.08	
5	.25	.23	.19	.16	.14	.13	.11	.10	.09	
6	.30	.27	.23	.19	.17	.15	.14	.12	.11	
7	.35	.32	.27	.23	.20	.18	.16	.14	.13	Legally Intoxicated
8	.40	.36	.30	.26	.23	.20	.18	.17	.15	
9	.45	.41	.34	.29	.26	.23	.20	.19	.17	Criminal Penalties
10	.51	.45	.38	.32	28	.25	.23	.21	.19	

Source: National Clearinghouse for Alcohol and Drug Information. http://ncadi.samhsa.gov; www.medicinenet.com.

problems. Drinking alcohol can make problems seem worse than they are. It often leads to **depression**, **anxiety**, and loneliness. Over time, the regular use of alcohol harms your body. Your liver, which removes poisons from the blood, is especially at risk. Alcohol also can damage your brain, kidneys,
and heart.

Alcohol is addictive. Each year, millions of Americans become alcoholics. An **alcoholic** loses the ability to control or stop drinking. **Alcoholism** is a **chronic** disease that gets worse over time.

People who start drinking alcohol at a young age are more likely to become alcoholics. Millions of teens become alcoholics before they are even old enough to legally drink alcohol. Cindy had her first drink at just 3 years old. By 14, she says, she knew what an alcoholic looked like. All she had to do was to look in the mirror.

CHAPTER THREE

Teen Drinking

A teen lies passed out on the sidewalk. Underage drinking laws have little effect on teen alcohol use.

Laws in the United States say you can't drink until you're 21 years old. Still, many people try alcohol when they are in their teens—or even younger. The Centers for Disease Control and Prevention (CDC) has studied this topic. In 2003, the CDC found, nearly 28 percent of U.S. students reported that their first drink of alcohol came before age 13. Other studies have shown that 80 percent of students have tried alcohol by the time they graduate from high school. Some of these teens drink alcohol often. Others consume alcohol rarely, but in huge quantities. Such **binge drinking** can be very dangerous.

Studies show similar drinking patterns among Canadian teens. In an Ontario

Learning & Innovation Skills

The United States has the highest legal drinking age in the world. In Canadian provinces, the drinking age is 19, with the exception of Quebec, where it is 18. In countries that have a legal drinking age, the most common age is 18. Many countries do not set an age limit. Among them are China, Portugal, and most of Poland.

Some Americans believe that the drinking age should be lowered to 18. You can vote at 18. You can fight for your country at 18. You are legally an adult at 18. What do you think? Should 18-year-olds be able to drink in the United States? Why or why not?

Binge drinking can be a serious problem for teenagers. Their bodies and brains are still developing and alcohol can interfere with that development.

study, 83 percent of 12th-grade students said they drink alcohol. Forty-five percent reported at least one episode of binge drinking in the previous four weeks. More than half of the students who drank said that drinking had caused them to feel sick, miss school or work, get arrested, or have a car accident.

Alcohol is particularly dangerous for young people because their brains and bodies are still growing. Students who drink alcohol find it harder to think clearly and to do well in school. Teens who use alcohol often have trouble making and keeping friends. They are more prone to fighting and other violent behavior, including suicide.

Experts have shown links between trying alcohol at a young age and **alcohol abuse** and alcoholism as an adult. The National Institute on Alcohol Abuse and

Life & Career Skills

In some schools, teens sneak alcoholic beverages into school events. Alcohol sometimes turns up at homecoming dances and football games. Some teens also follow up school parties by heading to a friend's house for a drinking party. What can schools do to discourage teens from drinking at and after school events? How can teachers and school officials address teen drinking at school events? How can students address this problem? What is the appropriate role for parents?

Waiting until age 21 to start drinking reduces the chance of developing a drinking problem.

Alcoholism has studied these links. It says that people who begin drinking before age 15 are *four times* more likely to develop alcohol **dependence** than those who begin drinking at age 21. Actress Drew Barrymore says she had her first drink at age 9. Her drinking led to a lot of problems. By age 12 she was doing cocaine and other hard drugs. Drew is one of many Hollywood stars who have gotten help for their addiction. Some drinkers have not been as lucky as Drew. Some have died from their addiction to alcohol.

CHAPTER FOUR

Solving Alcohol Abuse

Adults overindulge in alcohol at social events, including business functions.

Many adults wouldn't think of going to a concert or ball game without enjoying their favorite beverage. Some teens wouldn't think of going to a party without beer. But going to any event just because you're looking forward to drinking there is a warning sign. It's a sign of alcohol dependence. For many people, liking alcohol leads to dependence. Dependence leads to alcoholism.

Some people assume that alcoholics are easy to spot. They are the guys in ragged clothes asleep on a park bench with a paper bag under their arm, right?

Wrong. Alcoholics come in all ages and professions. They may be male or female, young or old. The one thing alcoholics share is a constant desire for alcohol. They also lack the ability to stop drinking once they start.

How do you know if someone you know has an alcohol problem? Alcohol abusers are often unpredictable. Their moods swing from happy to sad to angry. They might apologize after drinking for the things they said while drunk. Young people who start drinking sometimes abandon their old friends. They might hang out with a new crowd of kids. They may show little interest in activities they once enjoyed. Often, their grades drop and school becomes unimportant.

It's very hard for an alcoholic to stop drinking. It's even harder for an alcoholic to drink in moderation.

21st Century Content

It can sometimes be difficult to tell the difference between someone who enjoys alcohol occasionally and someone who is at risk of alcoholism. John Knight, a doctor at Boston Children's Hospital, designed the CRAFFT questionnaire to help you recognize warning signs for alcohol or drug abuse. Dr. Knight says that two or more yes answers indicates a significant problem.

- Have you ever ridden in a CAR driven by someone (including yourself) who was "high" or had been using alcohol or drugs?
- Do you ever use alcohol or drugs to RELAX, feel better about yourself, or fit in?
- Do you ever use alcohol/drugs while you are by yourself, ALONE?
- Do your family or FRIENDS ever tell you that you should cut down on your drinking or drug use?
- Do you ever FORGET things you did while using alcohol or drugs?
- Have you gotten into TROUBLE while you were using alcohol or drugs?

Solitary drinking is often a sign of alcohol addiction.

This is why so many alcoholics join support groups, such as Alcoholics Anonymous (AA). At AA meetings, alcoholics work together to overcome their addiction. Members work through a 12-step program on the path to recovery.

Organizations such as Alcoholics Anonymous can help alcoholics overcome their dependence on alcohol.

There are also support groups for families of alcoholics. Al-Anon and Alateen are perhaps the best known. Sixteen-year-old Jennifer says that Alateen helped her deal with some of the problems of having an alcoholic father. "It was good to hear that other kids had the same problems I did," Jennifer explains. "You realize you're not alone out there. You don't feel as weird."

Learning & Innovation Skills

The Internet is a valuable resource for people who want to learn more about alcohol-related problems. Several Web sites help people assess their risk without anyone knowing who they are. Visit the Web sites of some of the organizations listed at the back of this book. Then, use your computer's search engine to find other resources for alcoholics. What resources do you think would be most valuable for alcoholics? For their families? Why?

School counselors, teachers, and professional counselors are just a few of the many people that can help people deal with the problems that result from alcohol abuse. The good news is that anyone who has a problem with alcohol can stop if they get the right help. But the best idea of all is not starting in the first place!

CHAPTER FIVE

Making Good Choices

A student turns down a drink offered by a friend. Teens often drink because their friends drink.

"Who wants a drink? Try it—just one drink won't hurt you. You're not scared, are you?"

As you get older, you will probably be offered an alcoholic drink at some point. In this situation, the more

Students in West Burlington, Iowa, march in a Red Ribbon Week parade. The parade remembers those who died because of drunk driving.

knowledge you have, the more you'll be able to make the right choice. Here are some common reasons teens use alcohol, and good reasons not to.

Many young people first try alcohol because they think drinking is "grown-up." But drinking has nothing to do with being an adult. Many adults choose not to drink as part of a healthy lifestyle. Still others have never taken a sip of alcohol because their religion says not to.

Learning & Innovation Skills

Some people are more at risk of developing alcohol dependence than others. Here are a few of the risk factors:

Age: Alcohol and other drug use at an early age is one of the best indicators of future drug or alcohol problems.

Lack of information: Many teens are uninformed of the dangers of alcohol and do not realize that drinking too much too quickly can even lead to death.

Family ties: Children of alcoholics are three to four times more likely to become alcoholics than children of nonalcoholics.

Gender: Males are more likely than females to become dependent on alcohol, but alcohol has a stronger effect on women's bodies.

Ability to cope with problems: It can be tempting to deal with shyness, stress, family troubles, and other problems by drinking alcohol. But alcohol doesn't make these problems go away. In fact, it usually makes them worse.

Based on what you have learned about the risk factors, what can you do to help your friends avoid becoming dependent on alcohol?

Life & Career Skills

The Leadership to Keep Children Alcohol Free program offers these one-liner pressure busters to help you and your friends say no to alcohol without guilt or embarrassment:

Alcohol's NOT my thing.

No, thanks; I have better things to do!

I don't feel like it—do you have any soda?

Are you talking to me? FORGET it.

Why do you KEEP pressuring me when I've said NO?

Back off!

Many young people drink because their friends drink. It might seem like everyone is drinking, but this isn't true. In fact, most middle school kids—80 to 90 percent—don't drink alcohol. Look for friends who—like you—are interested in finding healthier ways to have fun.

It might seem cool to drink, until you think about it. There is nothing cool about throwing up or passing out.

It can be hard to say no when others around you are drinking. Some people might try to pressure you into joining in. Your real friends like you for who you are and will respect your decisions. If you don't want to try alcohol, say so. Stand tall, look directly at others, and say clearly, "No thanks." Be confident in your decision. If you sound unsure, others will be more likely to try to make you change your mind.

Waiting until adulthood to try new experiences such as drinking can lead to healthier long-term choices.

Perhaps you want to try drinking to see what it is like. It's normal to be curious about new things, especially if it seems like everyone is doing it. But you have plenty of time. Wait until you are an adult, when you are more likely to be able to handle the feelings—good and bad—that result.

Glossary

alcohol abuse (AL kuh hol uh BYOOS) harmful drinking practices involving alcohol

alcoholic (al kuh HOL ik) a person with alcoholism; made with alcohol

alcoholism (AL kuh hol izm) a disease of the body and mind in which a person is dependent on alcohol

alcohol poisoning (AL kuh hol POY zuh ning) serious illness or death caused by drinking too much alcohol

anxiety (ang ZIE uh tee) strong worry or nervous fear

at risk in danger of; having an increased chance for

binge drinking (BINJ DRINK ing) drinking a lot of alcohol in a short period of time, especially uncontrolled drinking

blood alcohol content the amount of alcohol in a person's blood; one way of testing whether a person is legally drunk

chronic (KRON ik) long-lasting; always present or occurring over and over

cocktail (KOK tayl) a drink that is made by mixing different beverages, usually including alcohol

dependence (di PEN dens) addiction to alcohol or drugs

depression (de PRESH uhn) an ongoing feeling of sadness and hopelessness, usually combined with poor concentration, lack of energy, and too much or too little sleep

drug an often addictive substance that causes changes in the body

fermented (fur MENT ed) made alcoholic by a chemical process in which yeast changes carbohydrates (mostly sugars and starches) into ethyl alcohol and by-products

hangover (HANG oh vur) an illness caused by drinking too much alcohol; common symptoms are headache, nausea, and thirst

Prohibition (proh hib BISH shun) the period of U.S. history, from 1919 to 1933, when the Eighteenth Amendment banned most making and selling of alcohol

spirits (SPEER its) alcoholic beverages made by distilling, or purifying, a liquid by boiling and cooling it

For More Information

Books

Aretha, David. *On the Rocks: Teens and Alcohol.* New York: Franklin Watts, 2007.

Bingham, Jane. *Alcohol.* Chicago: Heinemann, 2005.

Deboo, Anna. *Alcohol.* Chicago: Heinemann, 2007.

Jones, Penny. *Brown Bottle.* Center City, MN: Hazelden, 2004.

Levete, Sarah. *"Let's Talk About" Alcohol.* Mankato, MN: Stargazer, 2007.

Lynette, Rachel. *Alcohol (The Real Deal).* Chicago: Heinemann-Raintree, 2007.

Sanders, Pete, and Steve Myers. *Choices and Decisions: Drinking Alcohol.* Mankato, MN: Stargazer, 2005.

Web Sites

Al-Anon/Alateen

www.al-anon.alateen.org

Al-Anon provides help to and information for families and friends of alcoholics. Alateen is a recovery program for young people who have drinking problems.

Alcoholics Anonymous (AA)

www.aa.org

AA provides help to and information for more than 2 million members worldwide; the only requirement for membership is a desire to stop drinking.

The Cool Spot

www.thecoolspot.gov

Designed for young teens, this colorful U.S. government site has easy-to-understand information about alcohol and tips for dealing with the pressure to drink.

Mothers Against Drunk Driving (MADD)

www.madd.org

MADD works to stop drunk driving and to support the victims of drunk driving accidents. The site explains how volunteers of all ages can get involved.

National Council on Alcoholism and Drug Dependence

www.ncadd.org

Provides information and statistics on alcoholism and drug addiction. The site offers an online test for teens to see how alcohol is affecting their lives.

Index

About the Author

Lydia Bjornlund is a freelance writer in Virginia, where she lives with her husband, Gerry Hoetmer; their children, Jake and Sophia; and their two cats. She has written eight nonfiction books for children, mostly on American history and government topics. She also has written dozens of books and training materials for adults. Ms. Bjornlund holds a master's degree in education from Harvard University and a bachelor of arts degree from Williams College.